I0755986

FINISHING LINE PRESS
www.finishinglinepress.com

A Wild Ride

poems by

Louise Kantro

Finishing Line Press
Georgetown, Kentucky

A Wild Ride

ISBN 979-8-89990-511-7 First Edition

ACKNOWLEDGMENTS

The author offers grateful thanks the editors of the following publications in which these poems first appeared:

Arlijo / "Passing"
Borders and Boundaries / "Four Choices"
Doomer Anthology / "I Sit on the Couch Staring at the Wall"
Monterey Poetry Review / "Heroes" / "Sales Pitch" (under the title "How They
Do It")
R.KV.R.Y Quarterly / "Lost"
Rushing Through the Dark / "Tahrir Square, 2011"
Stanislaus Connections / "Bully I" / "Bully II" / "Family Separation" / "Let Us Gather Our Strength" / "You're Not Paranoid if …"

Publisher: Leah Huete de Maines
Editor: Christen Kincaid
Cover Art: Leah Younker
Author Photo: Sheila Knox
Cover Design: Elizabeth Maines McCleavy

Order online: www.finishinglinepress.com
also available on amazon.com

Author inquiries and mail orders:
Finishing Line Press
PO Box 1626
Georgetown, Kentucky 40324
USA

Contents

"A functioning, robust democracy requires a healthy, educated, participatory followership, and an educated, morally grounded leadership."
—Chinua Achebe, Writer

"We do not have to become heroes overnight. Just one step at a time, meeting each thing that comes up, seeing it is not as dreadful as it appeared, discovering we have the strength to stare it down."
—Eleanor Roosevelt

For Pain and Shame Linger

There must be many tellings
of the deaths, disappearances, atrocities
committed against many, many thousands

here and there and more and more and more,
discoveries, which, if stacked like stones
would be enough to construct many

hogans, kiiches, earth lodges, longhouses,
but not be large enough to house
the collective grief of victims

alongside the shame of those who forced
boarding schools upon children, tried to impose
their culture on proud people, denied

food, molested, and abused many,
many children and caused a multitude
of women, young and old, to disappear

who only now—finally—have established
summits, task forces, and executive orders
that report such crimes after the fact,

which falls far short of returning people alive
to those who love them but does not eradicate
the torch of hatred passed through generations.

In Canada, solar lanterns mark mass graves
of children. Photographic images—all those lights,
all those deaths—might be said to provide a salve

but let us not stop there and call it sufficient.
While such efforts acknowledge the suffering
and commemorate the dead by gathering

data, as Europeans do, about just how many
were from here, from there, died or were killed,
such reports cannot express the immensity

of the crushing pain.

I Sit on the Couch Staring at the Wall

November-December, 2024

Minimize	please don't
Discuss	please don't
Analyze	please don't
Hate	trying not to
Resent	trying not to
Blame	trying not to
Retreat	want to
Isolate	want to
Watch the news	not ready
Read headlines	sometimes

Breathe
Lay low
Wait

Family Separation

Alicia:
Papoosed against your mother
you trek for many months
and many miles.
The walking stops.
The wait begins.
You cry and cry
in the darkness.

After many more months and miles
you wake up in a bright-colored nursery.
You visit a nice lady
who calls you *speech-delayed.*
You are taken on play dates.
You begin to call the people
in the house
Mommy and Daddy.
A few years pass.
You can speak now
but mostly you are silent.

Esme:
In the coldest December
for thirty years,
you start at a new school.
The teacher seats you next
to Alicia, who has a nice smile
but is very quiet.
You speak no English.
She looks like she might speak Spanish
but when you try
she says nothing.
Unlike her, you remember
your parents and two brothers.

Bully—I

Please stop.
You keep riding ahead
then circling back on your bike
like a boomerang
to taunt me.
Mom says to ignore you
especially after school like this
when I'm walking home alone
so I look away,
pretend you're not there.
This makes you
madder, meaner.
You're scaring me now.
Don't turn around again
or jump the curb.
Go away!
The words catch in my throat.

The Wall

I'm Drew. I'm Flaco. I'm the kid who doesn't go to school or if I do I sit in the back, slouched down, letting everybody know I'm not interested in anything the teacher is talking about because the idiots who do participate need to know where I stand and to step back. Sometimes I get a little interested, but I stomp on it right away because school is stupid. And stop looking at me.

We write our names on walls, tunnels, trains, storefronts, garages, churches, anything with a wall because we don't like walls. We don't obey walls. But we do like our names and what we represent. Give us some spray, a knife, a sharpie and we can make our mark. Oh, and we like to see who else is on the wall because maybe they're like us.

I'm Drew. I'm Flaco. I'm 2Steaks. I'm Scott. I'm anybody who has written on this wall and I matter just as much as you do. You know, I don't see your name here.

Lost

You shun
calls, work, friends
night sleep
grooming
equilibrium
an actual job
and what you call
my need to control.

I fear
the loose robes
you wrap around
your hours
theft
collection agencies
car wrecks and
cocaine's seductive
lies.

But yet I hope.

Sales Pitch

Two nineteen-year-olds with
long, straight hair and dangly earrings,
we sit side by side in English class,
see each other one day in the cafeteria,
eat, talk, laugh, decide to meet again
the next Thursday after class.

I am working twenty hours a week
taking a full load of classes.
She hedges when I ask if she works, too.
Do you have a boyfriend?
No, I say. Focusing on school.

We meet one more time.
I make good money, she tells me,
pausing to look me over carefully.
I do sex, you know.
With guys. It pays for school
and an apartment.
You don't have to actually do it.
There are other things they like.
I could introduce you to someone.

Every Breath You Take

We know where you are. We know where you've been.
We can more or less know what you're thinking about.
—Eric Schmidt, former CEO of Google

The Good
Tracking devices on phones of teenagers & elders ease
the minds of worrying family members.
Cameras above doorsteps monitor from afar,
can be checked from thousands of miles away.
Talking voices warn porch-step visitors:
We know you're there. Do no wrong.
Surveillance cameras solve crimes.

The Bad
Ads for products that emerge after your recent
key word searches lurk at the sidelines
as you check email or online news.
Covenant Eyes ("Victory Over Porn is Possible!")
demands allegiance to a moral code.

The Ugly
A jealous boyfriend puts a tracking device
on your car, sells private sex tapes
for revenge or profit.
Racism and extremism spread like a virus online.
Catfishing can deceive anyone, even you.
Pro-anorexia and pro-suicide
chatrooms seduce the vulnerable.

Passing

In 1930: Black but with light skin
Meant family might suggest it's best you move
Even if it separated you from kin
If passing meant that life for you'd improve.

In 1950: If you wanted kids
Promotions, wife, an active social life
You learned to live your real life off the grid
Have secret same-sex "friends," avoiding strife.

In 1990: Secrets stole your voice.
You tried to seem just like your many friends
But Daddy made it clear you had no choice
For who'd believe you? Better to pretend.

To live what's false as truth exacts a cost
And shame won't ease the pain or all that's lost.

Bully—II

I just want to do my job.
Every day you seek me out,
get too close to me.
Even though I step back,
ask you to stop,
you persist, whispering
dirty words
explicit fantasies
cruel taunts.
I tell a few colleagues.
Some sympathize.
Some make excuses
for you or act
like I must be exaggerating.
I could go to HR
but, despite official policies,
going public would taint me.
What should I do?

Delayed Treatment

In Memory of Amber Nicole Thurman
(1993-2022)

She was young, with a six-year-old.
The timing was not right.
Her dogged goal a degree to hold.
Right now it seemed their futures bright.

It wasn't a good time to have a child.
She took the abortion pill.
At first her pains were mostly mild.
That's when her blood began to spill.

She called for help at the hospital.
They firmly turned her away.
Though things got worse, even critical
State law said they had to keep her at bay.

Back home, she felt her pains increase.
Again, she sought relief.
But the cramps hurt bad and did not cease.
Three ER visits resulted in grief.

It was no aisling, no dream, but real.
Not yet thirty, she died.
A woman's right they did willfully steal,
Left mother, sister, and son to cry.

Stand Back and Stand By

Rough as leathery skin

raw as a straight shot of whiskey
we are the only true Americans.

Proud of our independence
our rough-ridin' cowboy ways
we will not be corralled.

It infuriates us when others
claim the privilege
of being one of us.
We ridicule people who

get in our faces
don't learn English
think they belong here.
We mock anyone outside our circle.
We will not hesitate

to raise our fists—or our AK-47's.
Feel free to stereotype us.
We'd be glad to exaggerate our ways
if it will get your goat.
We are gaining in number.
And we are loud.

You're Not Paranoid if …

I feel it
in my solar plexus
like a complaining ulcer
with its churning and growling
my limbs paralyzed
with the dream-force
of *I-can't-move*
in a realm like
Putin's, Kim Jong-un's, Orban's
only here, here.

I stepped off
a plane in Budapest
a year ago, knowing
I was now in a country controlled
by an autocrat. How normal
it seemed with stores and restaurants,
public transportation,
sidewalk sweepers, friendly people.

I worry about my country's
global loss of respect
and, yes, status,
but mostly I fear
being thrust
into a Stepford Wives
lock-step, where I pretend
all is well but the hairs
on my arms bristle
every time I walk outside,
afraid of being monitored for loyalty,
watched to see if I am out-of-step.

Trauma

1.

You were just goofing around,
you and your buddies,
your best friend's little sister
hanging around, unwanted,
like she always did.
You grabbed the gun.
It went off.

You still had to go to school.
Everyone knew.
Everyone looked at you.
No one talked to you.
You went to court and were cleared.
Your family moved to another town.
For you.
They moved for you.

2.

Shot in the head at twelve means
headaches almost every day
that you hate fireworks
that you became an introvert.
Were you before? You can't remember.
It doesn't help that the kid lied,
said he hadn't aimed at you
when he had, which doesn't mean
he actually wanted to hurt you,
but that he lied means
who can you trust?

Anthem for The Discouraged

Mine eyes have seen the glory
Of the coming of the Lord
—Julia Ward Howe

We won't pander favor from you,
John Locke and Adam Smith.
Your manifestos included dynamic pricing,
dictated by supply and demand,
policies that make sense but lack empathy
or pathways out of poverty.
At what point does allision,
say, of the bridge in Baltimore, Maryland
mean we should not simply scrap
the allure of lore and theory and get down
to the business of repairing the damage,
no matter the number of hours or cost?
You two economy "experts" lie
demurely in your graves while, working
together, we manage to open the port
in a mere three months, though full repair
of the Francis Scott Key Bridge
will take up to ten long years.

Democracy in the US may take longer
than a decade to repair
and may never return to its glory,
though blatantly racist Jim Crow Laws
and robber-baron polarization
can hardly be considered glorious.
While the country has had its noble moments,
for this Great American Experiment
to become the righteously glorious
country envisioned by the Founders,
we need to get over seeing ourselves
as the world's beacon of light.
Let us *sound the trumpet that shall never call retreat*

and with patience, persistence, and chutzpah,
let us gather, talk, shape a better and stronger
country from the ashes of the old.

Shattered Glass

Once I dropped
a pickle jar
the kind with pieces
of garlic in the brine
and it scared you,
that noise, but mostly
it was the edge
you heard in my voice
as I tried to calm you
by tossing Cheerios
onto your highchair tray.
It took me ten minutes
to sweep the shards
into a dustpan
then the trash.
Three rounds of mopping
and still the kitchen stank
and our shoes stuck
to the floor for a week.

How many mothers
had to ignore their babies' cries
to tend gently to their fathers
whose old bones and spirits
were shattered like
store windows on that
cold, cold November in
Germany in 1938.

Four Choices

He writes about the cusp of time
before anyone knew the Nazis would lose.
It was a time when people had four
and, according to him, only four choices
of who to be:
bully, coward, victim, or rebel.
You could be one and then another
but never two at once.
The odd thread of connection
among these four roles
spurs him to return to write about
this time, this subject, this place,
over and over
again and again.

How the Brave Withstand: Ukraine, 2022

They wait and wait inside their cherished town.
They fight to save their homes from burning down.
With brave persistence, fighting hand to hand,
They see no other way but to take a stand.
Their children meanwhile shelter underground.

They wait and wait inside their cherished town
To hear from friends for help but feel let down.
Because of tanks, it's hard to cross the land.
Invaders see just how the brave withstand.

Exploding bombs soon bring huge buildings down.
They wait and wait inside their cherished town.
What more will come their way that can't be banned?
Their hopes, their dreams can hardly go as planned.
A road now opens, children can leave town
With mothers, dazed and numb, to safer land.

Tahrir Square, 2011

Though you wear the veil
as an emblem of your faith
you have learned to expect
that if you protest,
it will be ripped
from your face
leaving you exposed
like the blue bra
that showed through
after your beating,
after you were dragged
through the streets,
assaulted with hateful epithets,
some of them sexual.

There are those who think
women like you
don't deserve
the job
the recognition
the joy of accomplishment,
those who find it abhorrent
if you speak
if you act
if even a flicker
of protest shows
in your eyes
your brow
your shoulders.

There is a time
to veil
to mask
to strategize
to find their weaknesses
to stay in the shadows.

There is a time
to make your declaration.

Let Us Gather Our Strength

We thought we saw progress—
A Black President elected
Statues of Civil War secessionists dismantled
Gay marriage legalized
Diversity of all kinds in the military
Attempts to hold even the powerful accountable.

They broke my faith.
They broke your faith.
They broke our faith.

Pass the healing salve.
Massage the aching back.
Drink the broth.
One day soon we will
Stand up, rise up, stand up once again.
It's not yet time, but we will know
When to act and what to do.

They call all we want to do "woke"
Claim there were good things about slavery
Promise to get rid of "favoritism" for minorities
Purge the military of gay and Transgender troops
Give women's reproductive choice to the government
Line the pockets of the rich.

They broke my faith.
They broke your faith.
They broke our faith.

Pass the healing salve.
Massage the aching back.
Drink the broth.
One day soon we will
Stand up, rise up, stand up once again.
It's not yet time, but we will know
When to act and what to do.

Poise and Dignity

Like a statue of Athena
or the Virgin Mary,
your demeanor calm,
you look out at this circle
of male faces as they snarl—
Are you a scorned woman?
Do you have a militant attitude?
Do you have a martyr complex?
Are you interested in writing a book?
And nobody but you has come forward?
*Do you have anything to gain?**

Thank you, Anita, for speaking out
against your former boss, Judge Thomas.
The Senators' questions expose them
as privileged and bigoted
men who show little empathy
and a bizarre lack of decorum.

*Actual questions asked at the Senate hearing

When It's Personal

In our bridge foursome, we focus
on playing cards. We don't talk politics.
When there are lapses, we are civil,
but on those days, I go home in a bit of a mood.

Last week, our fourth, a substitute player,
political persuasion unknown,
told us her grandchild identifies
now as Transgender, born a girl,
now a boy with a gender-neutral name.
It's been hard for everyone
in the family to get used to
(she didn't say 'accept,'
but we can read between the lines).
She loves the child.
She can't quite say *him*,
but she's getting there, they all are.

I looked around the table.
Politics had not muscled
into the room.
I saw only grandparents
who could not imagine
un-loving a grandchild.

Heroes

"The arc of the moral universe is long,
but it bends toward justice."
—Theodore Parker, Abolitionist

1.

They, once respected and honored,
whose likenesses now evoke visceral
reactions of confusion, fear, hatred, disgust
for their role in dismantling a nation,
for seeing nothing wrong with enslaving people,
now face having statues bearing their names
toppled in rage or by dispassionate official decree.
Are they turning over in their graves,
embarrassed by this public humiliation
or puzzled at being expected
to feel shame, though if they examined
their words and actions, once so admired
and, sadly, still venerated by some,
they might see that their principles were birthed
from a profane and unholy place.

2.

You might never know in your lifetime
if the home, church, after-school program
you attended will become
a shrine or museum open for the public
to learn about what made you, you
or what the circumstances of your protests
now mean to those who yearn to honor and follow
your convictions, teachings, courage, and influence
by commemorating spaces you inhabited:
  The bus stop where Rosa Parks boarded.
  The Colored sections of bus stations.
  The 16th Street Baptist Church.
  The Edmund Pettis Bridge.
  The Woolworth's lunch counter.
  The Birmingham jailhouse.
  Soil under trees where ropes once hung.

A Wild Ride

Someone gave them the key to my dream so all seven of them, like teenagers in a 1960's movie, squeeze into a long and spacious car, maybe a Chevy or Cadillac, sitting three in the front and the rest touching shoulders in the back. Shoving each other playfully, their raucousness feels like they're just this much short of being delinquents—not like they're heading out to smoke crack but more like they're itchy-restless, even fearless as they egg each other on. Let's do this, no, that, and somehow the driver, probably the oldest at about nineteen, steers the car to do what three of them want, which is to go to a rave. Unintentional socialists, they pool their money to make it happen for all of them.

Somehow I know they're all foster kids, but they're not acting at all like the kids I work with who have been in the system two, five, nine years, whose personalities range from extrovert to introvert yet even the natural extroverts tend to stay under the radar, and they don't make friends easily, so how did seven find each other and they all just happen to be foster kids? I'm uneasy about these kids in ways I'm not with the real ones I know and wonder if it's because this group has so successfully tossed away the doubts, uncertainties, and anxieties that previously obstructed them by transferring them to me. I know down to my bones the odds that they will trust too much or too little; seek too much stimulation or its alternative, numbness; become homeless; go to jail; die young.

Louise Kantro, a retired high school English teacher, bridge-player, cat-lover, and CASA (Court Appointed Special Advocate) for foster children, received her MFA in Creative Writing from Goddard College in 2003, with an emphasis on short fiction.

For the past twenty years, she has focused on poetry, though she still writes some prose, publishing in both local and national journals. Her poem "Displacement of Loss" won the Derick Burleson Award in 2022, was published in The Best of Choeofpleirn, and was nominated for Best American Poetry. Her chapbook *Dwellingplaces* was published by Pudding House Press in 2010.

Her writing centers mostly around people and social issues. She is active in North-Central California poetry circles, currently serves as president of her local chapter of the National League of American Pen Women, and gets her ideas from scanning old photos, overheard conversations in coffee shops, and the news.

Poetry, reading, her grown children, husband, and friends sustain her in a world that gets crazier by the day.

www.ingramcontent.com/pod-product-compliance
Lightning Source LLC
LaVergne TN
LVHW090540110826
845146LV00003B/1202
* 9 7 9 8 8 9 9 9 0 5 1 1 7 *